SPECIAL-EFFECTS AND TOPICAL ALPHABETS

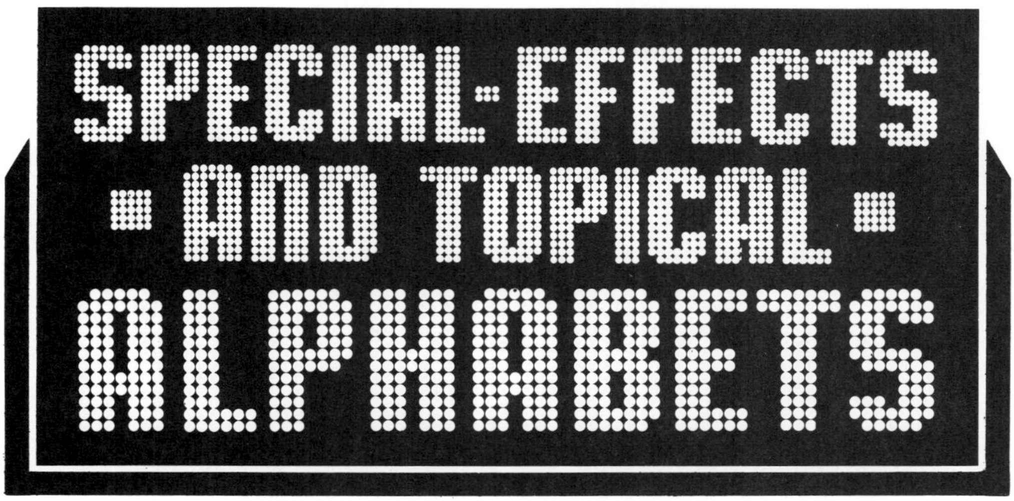

100 COMPLETE FONTS

SELECTED AND ARRANGED BY

DAN X. SOLO

FROM THE
SOLOTYPE TYPOGRAPHERS CATALOG

DOVER PUBLICATIONS, INC. · NEW YORK

Published in Canada by General Publishing Company, Ltd., 30 Lesmill Road, Don Mills, Toronto, Ontario.
Published in the United Kingdom by Constable and Company, Ltd.

Special-Effects and Topical Alphabets: 100 Complete Fonts is a new work, first published by Dover Publications, Inc., in 1978. The typefaces shown were selected and arranged by Dan X. Solo from the Solotype Typographers Catalog.

DOVER *Pictorial Archive* SERIES

International Standard Book Number: 0-486-23657-9
Library of Congress Catalog Card Number: 78-52150

Manufactured in the United States of America
Dover Publications, Inc.
31 East 2nd Street
Mineola, N.Y. 11501

ALDERWOOD

ABCDEFGHI
JKLMNOPQRS
TUVWXYZ&

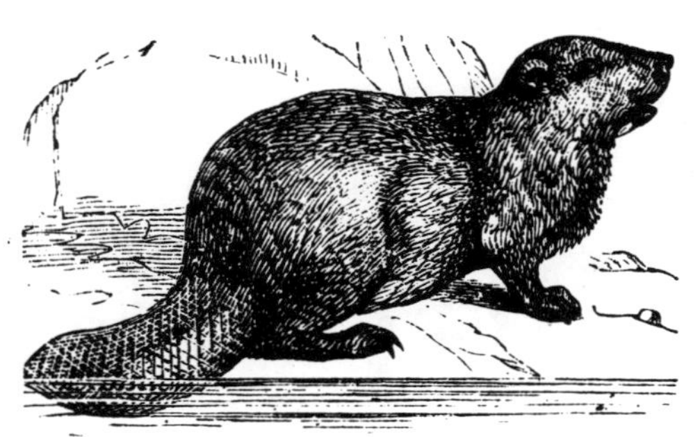

(&:;-’‘!?$¢)
1234567890

Arrowhead

ABCDEFGHIJ
KLMNOPQR
STUVWXYZ
(&:;-‘’!?$¢%)
abcdefghijklm
nopqrstuvwxyz
1234567890

AUTOMATION SHADED

AABCDDEEF
GHIJKLMNOPQ
RSTUVWXYZ

[&:;-'"!?$¢%]
1234567890

AZTECA

ABCDEFG
HIJKLMNO
PQRSTUV
WXYZ

(&:;-'"!?$¢%)
123
4567890

BOND SHADED

ABCDEFGHI
JKLMNOPQR
STUVWXYZ

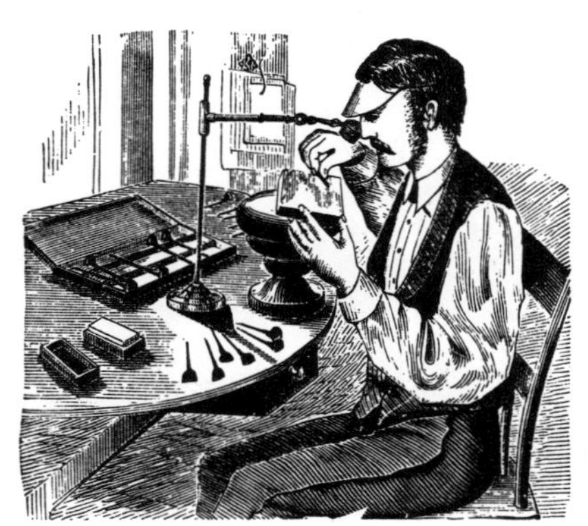

1234567890
(&:;-''!?$¢£)

Broken Bow

ABCDEFGH
IJKLM
NOPQR
STUVWXYZ
abcdefghij
klmnopqrstu
vwxyz
1234567890
(&:;-''!?¢$)

bunny ears

abbcdeffgh

hijkkllmnop

qrstuvvwxyz

&

12234567890

(:;-!?$&)

BURLAP

ABCDEFGH

IJKLMNOP

QRRSSTU

VWXYZST

rT

(&:;!?$)

1234567890

BURST

ABCDEFG
HIJKLMNO
PQRSSTU
VWXYZ

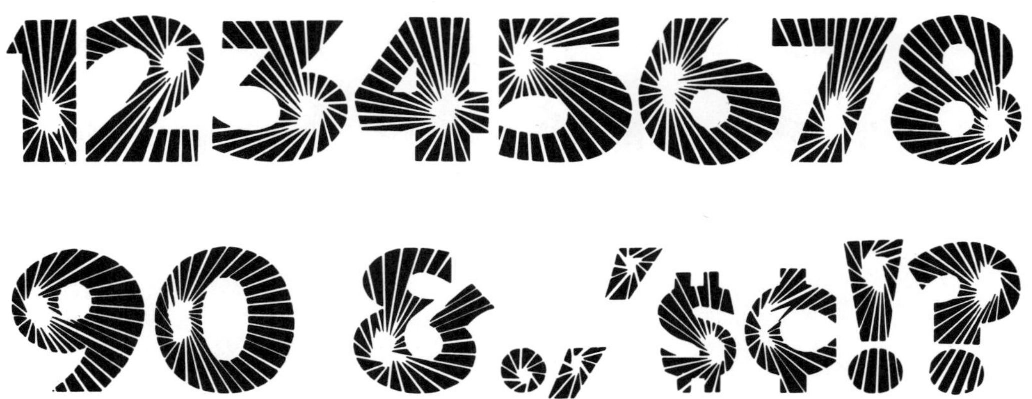

CAMPAIGN

A B C D E F G H

I J K L M N O

P Q R S T U V W

X Y Z

& : ' " " ! ? $

1 2

3 4 5 6 7 8 9 0

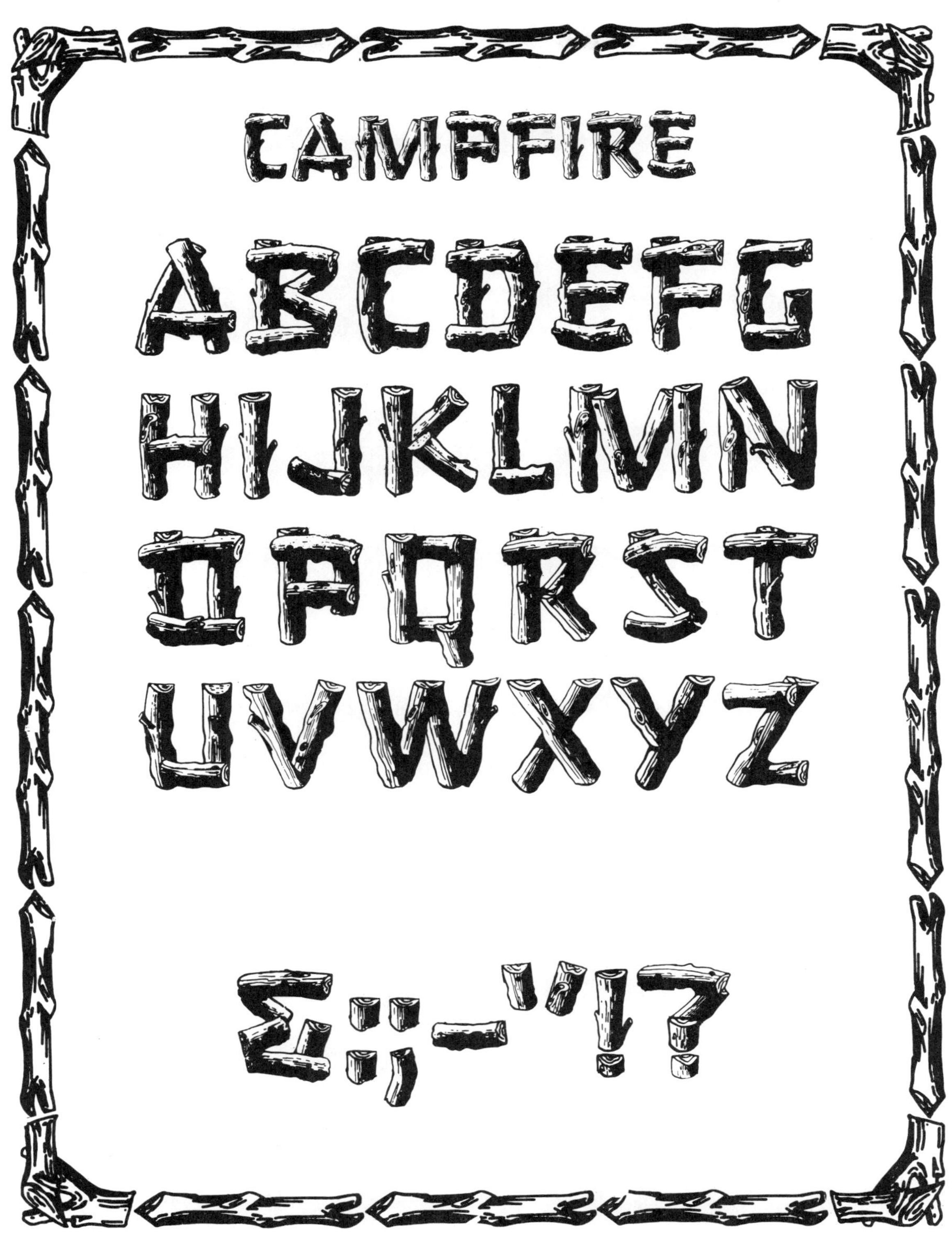
CAMPFIRE
ABCDEFG
HIJKLMN
OPQRST
UVWXYZ
&:;-"!?

CHALKBOARD

ABCDEFG

HIJKLMNO

PQRSTUV

WXYZ

&:;—''!?$¢

123

4567890

Chinatown

ABCDEFGHI
JKLMNOPQR
STUVWXYZ
&:;"!?¢$

abcdefghijklmn
opqrstuvwxyz

1234567890

Chopstick

ABCDEFGHI
JKLMNOPQRST
UVWXYZ

abcdefghijklmno
pqrstuvwxyz

CHUBBY

ABCDEFG
HIJKLM
NOPQRSTU
VWXYZ
&:;'!?
12
34567890

Colonial Dame

ABCDEFGH
IJKLMNOPQR
STUVWXYZ

abcdefghijklmn
opqrstuvwxyz

(&:;-‘’!?$¢)
1234567890

Colonial Dame Shaded

ABCDEFGHI
JKLMNOPQRS
TUVWXYZ
(&:;-''!?$¢)

abcdefghijklmno
pqrstuvwxyz

1234567890

COMIC BOOK

ABCDEFGHI
JKLMNOPQRS
TUVWXYZ&

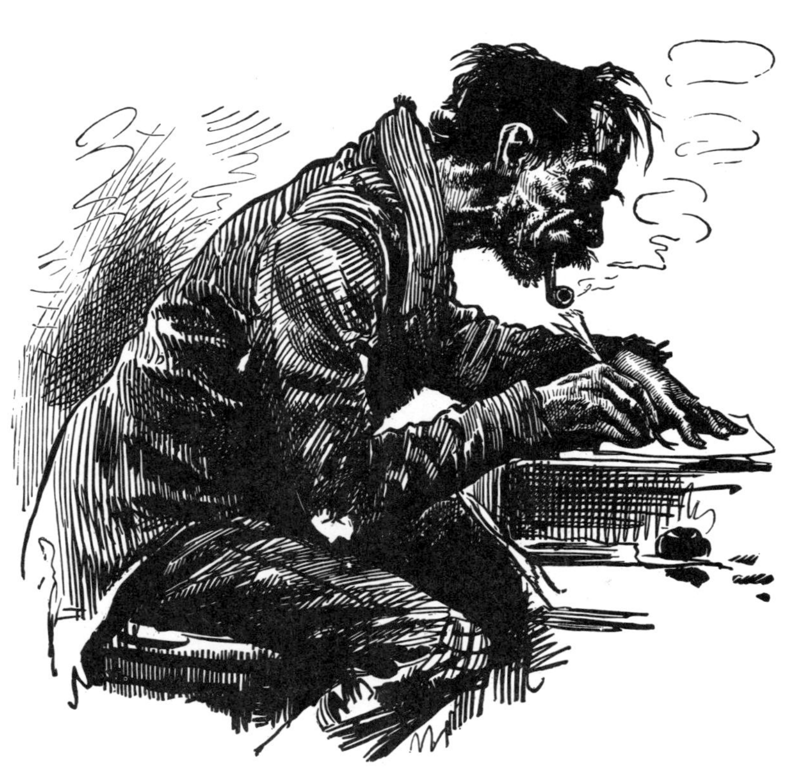

COMPUTER

ABCDEFGHI
JKLMNOPQR
STUVWXYZ

1234567890
[&:;-"!?$¢%]

CONFUCIUS

ABCDEFGH

IJKLMNOP

QRSTUVW

XYZ&:;-''!?

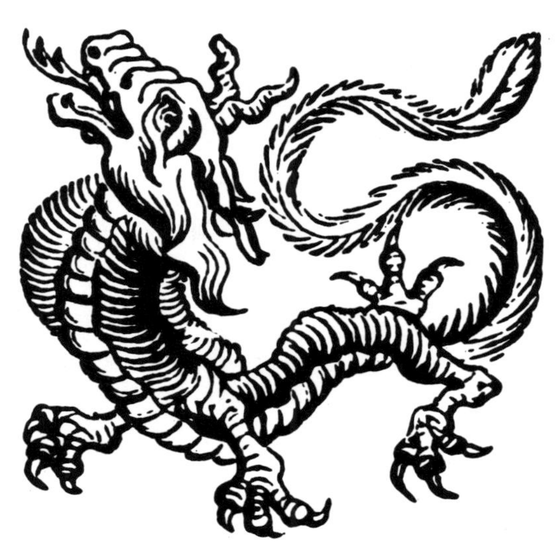

DAISYLAND

aaBCDDeeFG

HIIJKLLMNNO

OOPQRRRSST

TUUVWXYZ

12345678900

(&:;-'!?*$£¢)

DIMENSION 3

ABCDEFG

HIJKLMNO

PQRSTUV

WXYZ

&.,:;-'!?$¢

1234567890

DIRECTION

ABCDEFGHI
JKLMNOPQR
STUVWXYZ

1234567890
(&:;-"'!?$¢%)

Dominican

ABCDEFGH
IJKLMNOPQR
STUVWXYZ

(&:;-‘’!?$¢)

abcctdefghijklm
nopqrsſtuvwxyz

1234567890

DOPPLER

ABCDEFG

HIJKLMN

OPQRSTU

VWXYZ&

12345678

9 :;-''! 0

DRACULA SERIES

ABCDEFGH
IJKLMNOPQRS
TUVWXYZ

1234567890
(&:;-'!?$¢)

DRIFTWOOD

ABCDEFGHI
JKLMNOPQRS
TUVWXYZ

&:;-'!?$¢
1234567890

EXPLOSION

A A B C D E E F G

H I I J K K L L M

N N O O P Q R R

S S T T U V W X Y

Z

1 2 3 4 5 6 7 8 9 0

(& ; – ' ? ! $)

FADEOUT

ABCDEFG

HIJKLMNOP

QRSTUV

WXYZ

&:;"-?!¢$

123456789

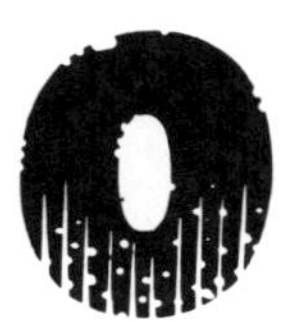

FANTAN

ABCDEFGHI
JKLMNOPQRS
TUVWXYZ

(&:;-*"!?¥¢$)
1234567890

Faust Text

ABCDEFGHI
JKLMNOPQRS
TUVWXYZ
(&.:;-''!?$)

abcdefghijklm
nopqrstuvwxyz
1234567890

FILM

ABCDEFG

HIJKLMN

OPQRSTU

VWXYZ&Z

ÆI2Œ

34567890

FIREBUG

ABCDEFG
HIJKLMNOPQ
RSTUVWXYZ

&:;-'!?

1234567890

FLAMO

ABCDEFGH
IJKLMNO
PQRS/
TUVWXYZ
(&:;''$ç?!)
1234567
890

Flex Ribbon

ABCDEFGHI
JKLMNOPQR
STUVWXYZ

abcdefghijklm
nopqrstuvwxyz

1234567890
(&:;-"!?$£)

FLINTSTONE

ABCDEFG
HIJKLMNOP
QRSTTUV
WXYZ

1234567890
(&.:;-'"!?$¢%)

FOCUS

ABCDEFG

HIJKLMN

OPQRST

UVWXYZ

1234567

890:;?!$

&

FRANKENSTEIN

ABCDEFGHI
JKLMNOPQRS
TUVWXYZ
1234567890
(&:;-''!?$¢)

Geometric Light

ABCDEFGH
IJKLMNOPQR
STUVWXYZ

abcdefghijklmn
opqrstuvwxyz

*

1234567890

(&;:-'"!?$%)

GROG CAPS

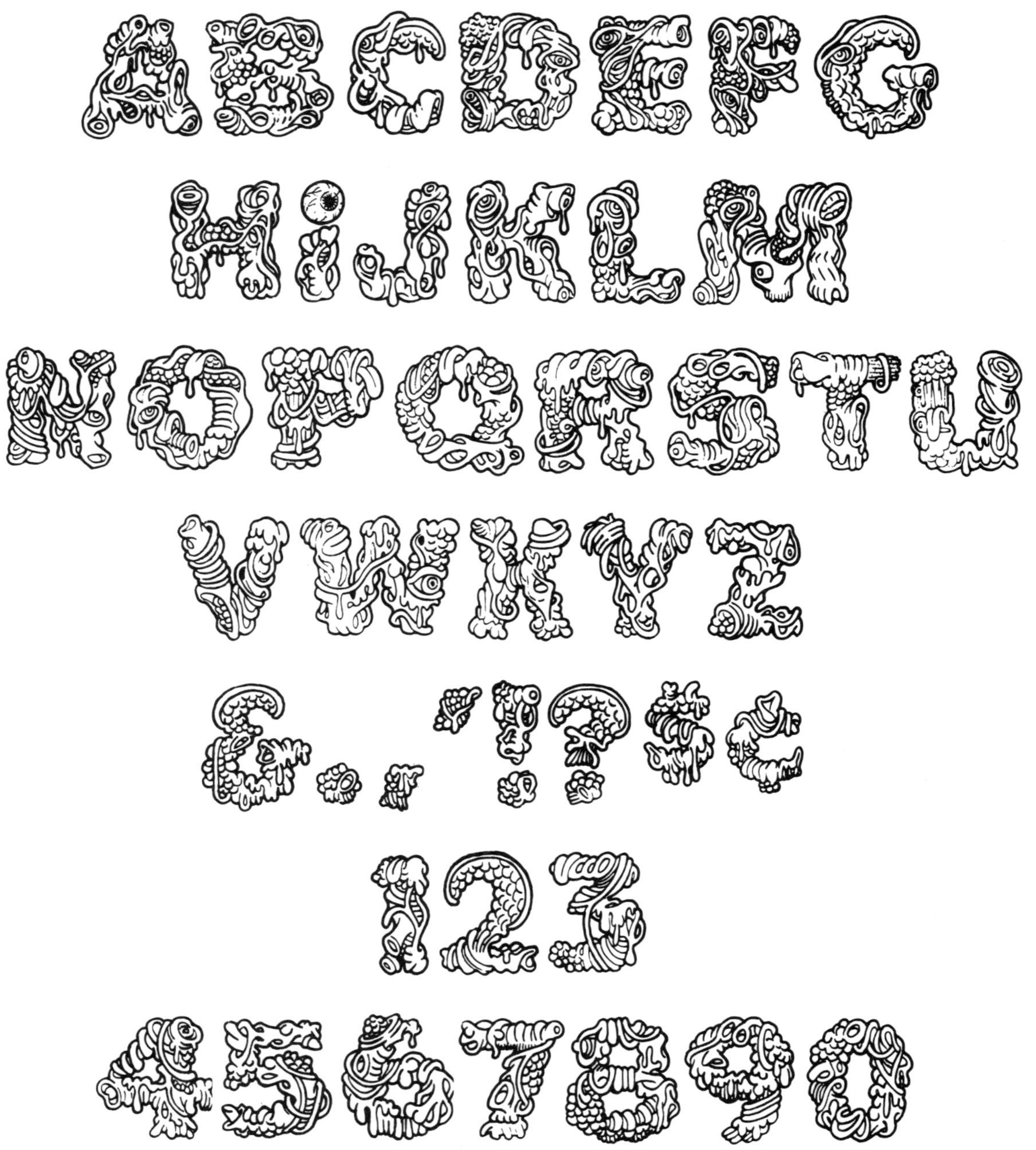

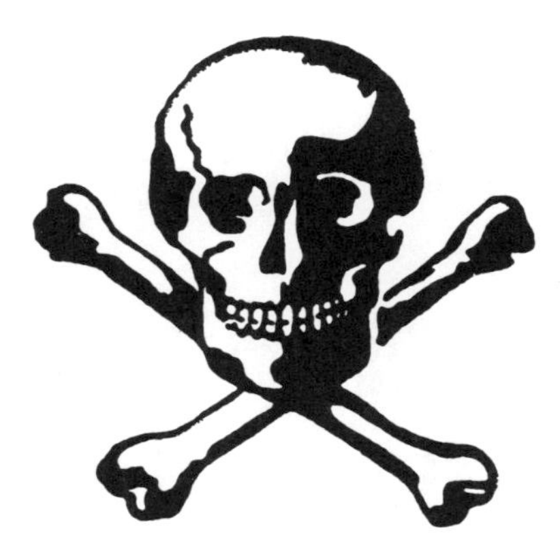

ABCDEFGHI
JKLMNOPQR
STUVWYZ
&:;-"!?

HEADHUNTER

HOLLYWOOD LIGHTS

ABCDEFGHI

JKLMNOPQR

STUVWXYZ

(&:;-'!?$¢%)

1234567890

HOLLYWOOD STARS

ABCDEFGH
IJKLMNOPQR
STUVWXYZ

1234567890
(&:;'"!?$¢%)

Home Sweet Home

ABCDEFGHIJK
LMNOPQRSTU
VWXYZ

abcdefghijklmno
pqrstuvwxyz

1234567890
(&:;-'!?$¢)

Icicle

ABCDEFGHI
JKLMNOPQR
STUVWXYZ

(&:;-''!?$¢)

abcdefgh
ijklmnopqrs
tuvwxyz

1234567890

IDEOGRAPH

ABCDEEF
GHHIIJJ
KLLMNNO
OPQRSSTE
UVWXYZ

1234567890
&.:,;"-!?$¢

IGLOO SOLID

ABCDEFGH
IJKLMNOPQR
STUVWXYZ

1234567890
&:;-''!?$¢

Import

ABCDEFGHI
JKLMNOPQR
STUVWXYZ

(&:;-’‘!?$)

abcdefghijkl
mnopqrst
uvwxyz

1234567890

INVISIBLE

ABCDEFG

HIJKLM

NOPQRSTU

VWXYZ

(&;:''!?$¢£%)

123456

7890

JIMINY CHRISTMAS

ABCDEFGHIJ

KLMNOPQR

STUVWXYZ

&:;-''!?$

1234567890

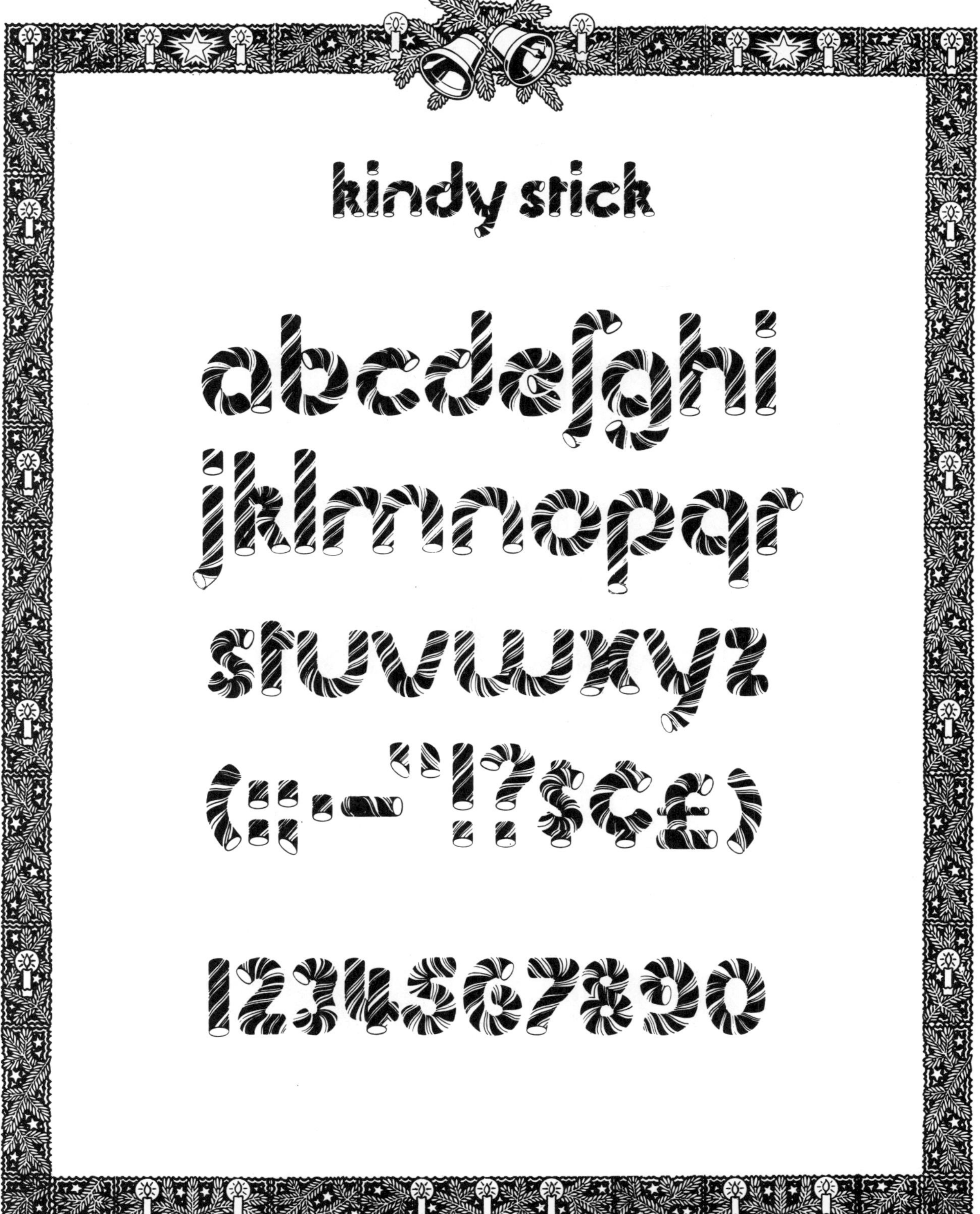
kindy stick
abcdefghi
jklmnopqr
stuvwxyz
(:;-—"!?$¢£)
1234567890

Lariat

ABCDEFGHIJ

KLMNOP

QRSTUVWXYZ

(&:;-'!?$)

abcdefghijklmno

pqrstuvwxyz

1234567890

MOSAIC GOTHIC

ABCDEFGH
IJKLMN
OPQRSTU
VWXYZ
(&:;-'!?$)

12
34567890

MOSES CONDENSED

ABCDEFGH
IJKLMNOPQR
STUVWXYZ

1234567890
(&:;-‘’!?$¢%)

MOSKOW

ABCDEEFG
HIJKLMN
OΦPQЯRST
ЦVШXYЗZ

1234567890

(&:;-'!?$¢%)

NATIONAL SPIRIT

ABCDEFGH
IJKLMNOPQR
STUVWXYZ

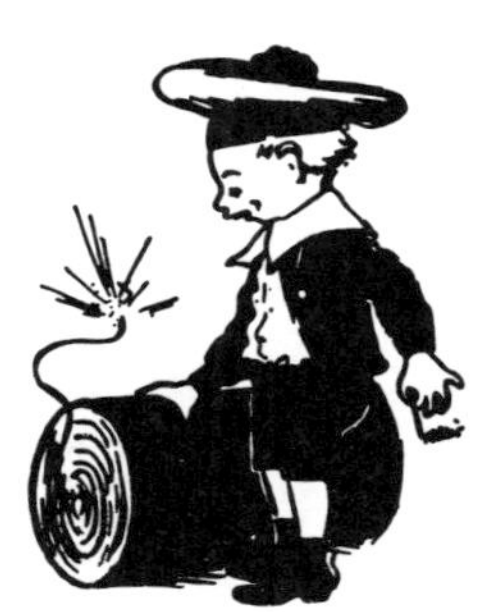

1234567890
:;-'"!?

NECKTIE STRIPED

ABCDEFG

HIJKLMNOPQR

STUVWXYZ

1234567890

&.,:;-'!?—$

Needlepoint

ABCDEFGH
IJKLMNOPQR
STUVWXYZ
[&:;-'"!?$¢%/]
abcdefghijkl
mnopqrst
uvwxyz
1234567890

Old German

ABCDEFGHI
JKLMNOPQRS
TUVWXYZ
(&:;'!?)

abcdefghijklmnop
qrstuvwxyz

1234567890

OLD GLORY

ABCDEFGHI
JKLMNOPQRS
TUVWXYZ
&:;-"!?$

1234567890

Pencraft Text

ABCDEFGH
IJKLMNOPQRS
TUVWXYZ

abcdefghijklmnop
qrstuvwxyz

1234567890
(&:;-“”!?$¢)

PINBALL

ABCDEFGH

IJKLMNOPQRS

TUVWXYZ

(&.;-'"!?$£)

abcdefghijklmno

pqrstuvwxyz

1234567890

PINWHEEL GOTHIC

ABCDEFGHI

JKLMNOPQR

STUVWXYZ

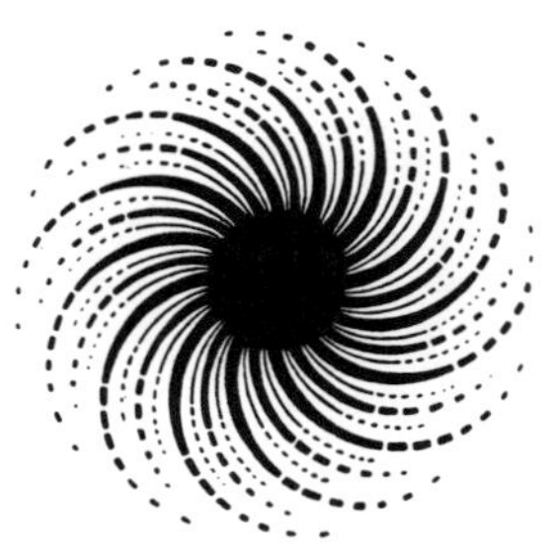

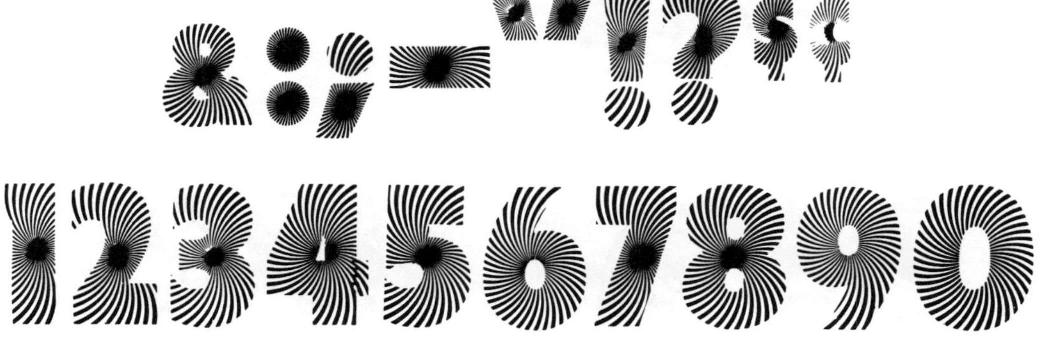

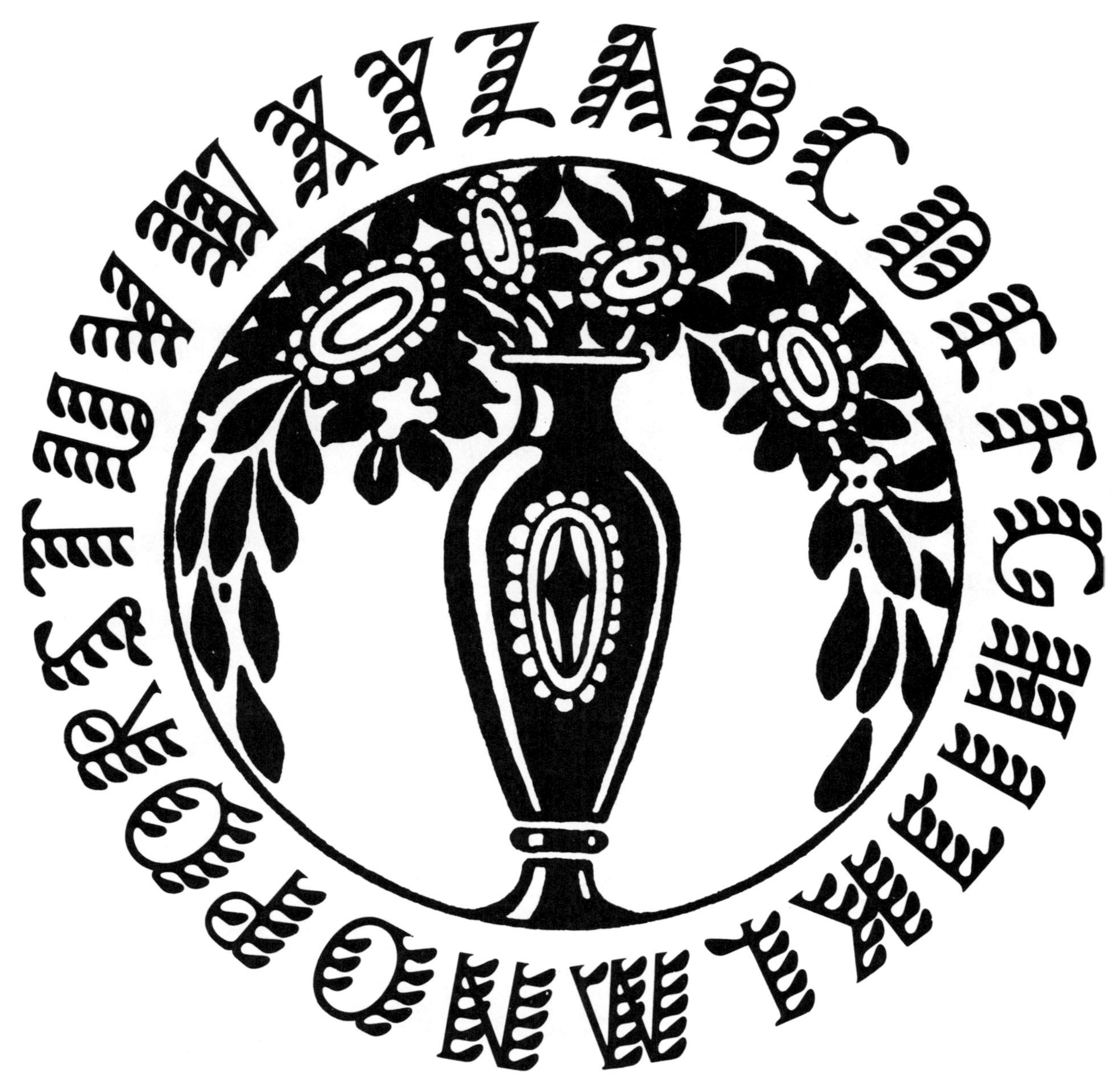

POLLY

PROTEST

AABCDEEF
GHIIJKLLMN
NOOPQRRSS
TTUVWXYZ

1234567890
(&:;-'!?$¢£%)

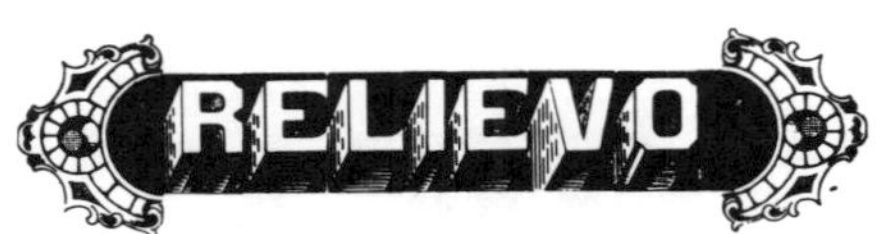
RELIEVO

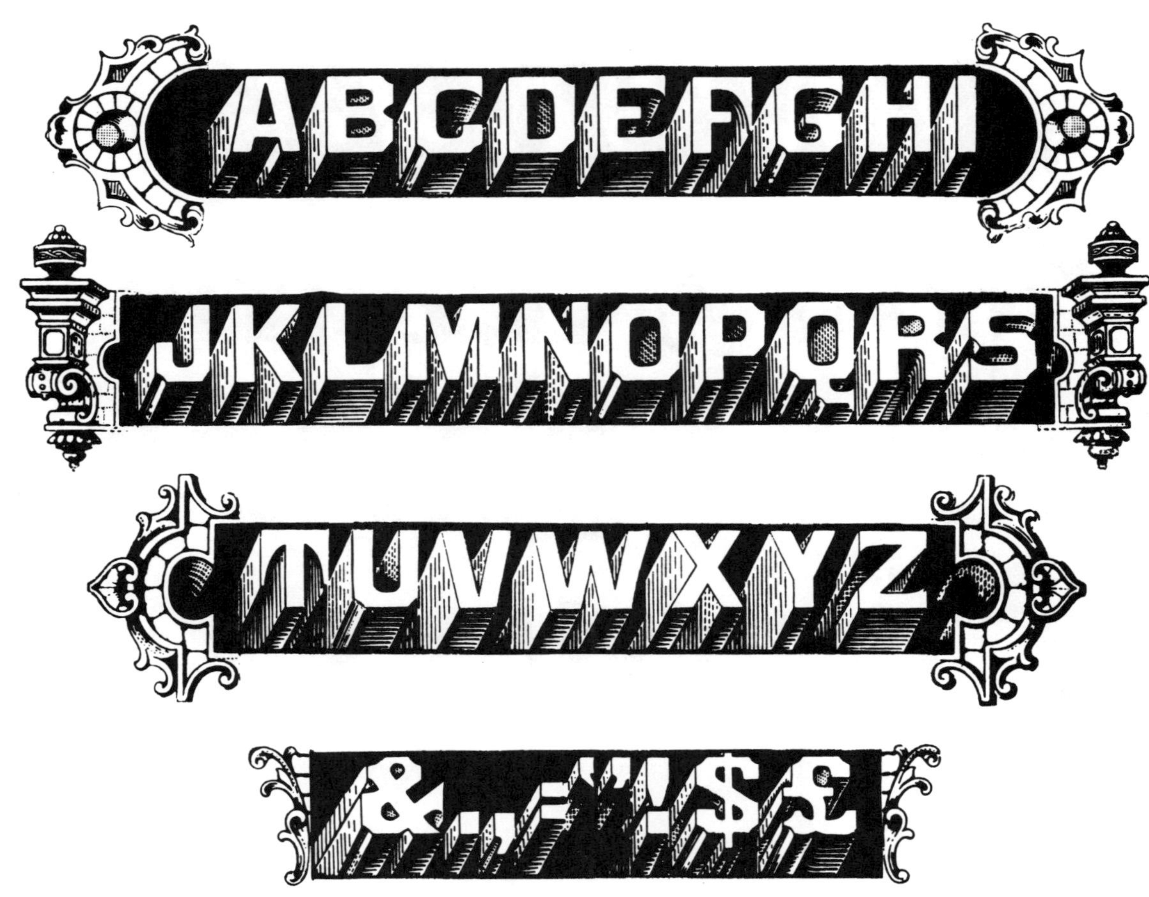
ABCDEFGHI
JKLMNOPQRS
TUVWXYZ
&.,-"!$£

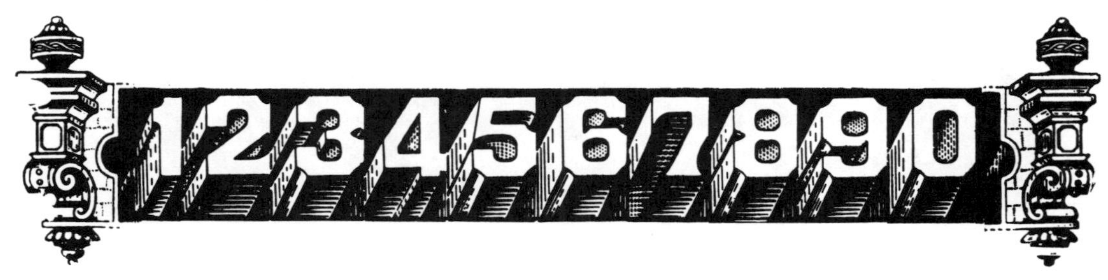
1234567890

Ribbonfaced Typewriter

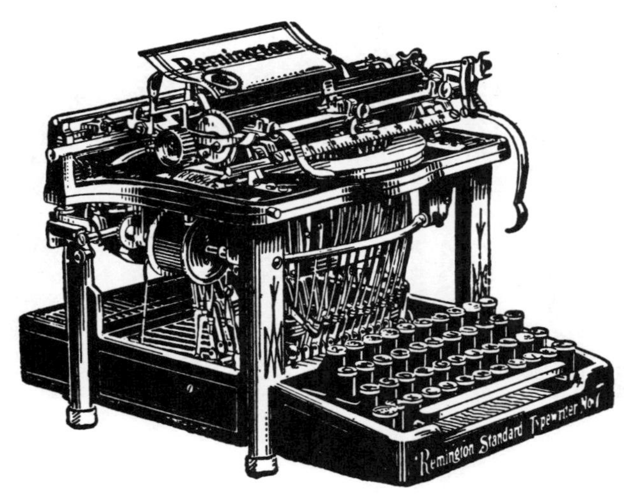

ABCDEFGHIJKLMN
OPQRSTUVWXYZ
(&:;-'"!?$¢)
abcdefghijklmno
pqrstuvwxyz
1234567890

RIPTIDE

ABCDEFGH

IJKLMNOPQR

STUVWXYZ

.?!,

$¢£%

1234567890

RUSTIC

ABCDEFGH
IJKLMNOPQR
STUVWXYZ

(&:;-'!?$£)
1234567890

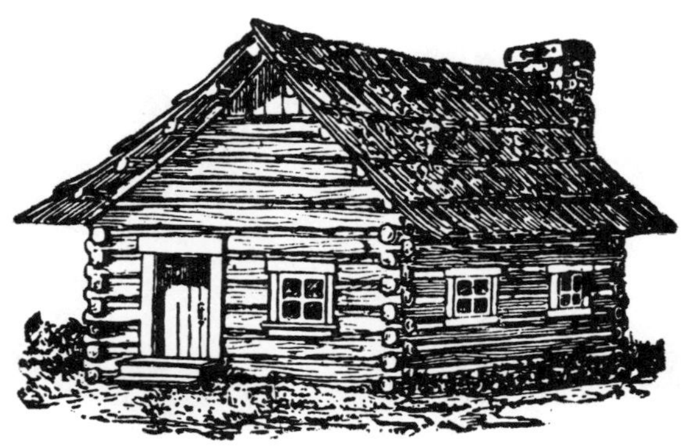

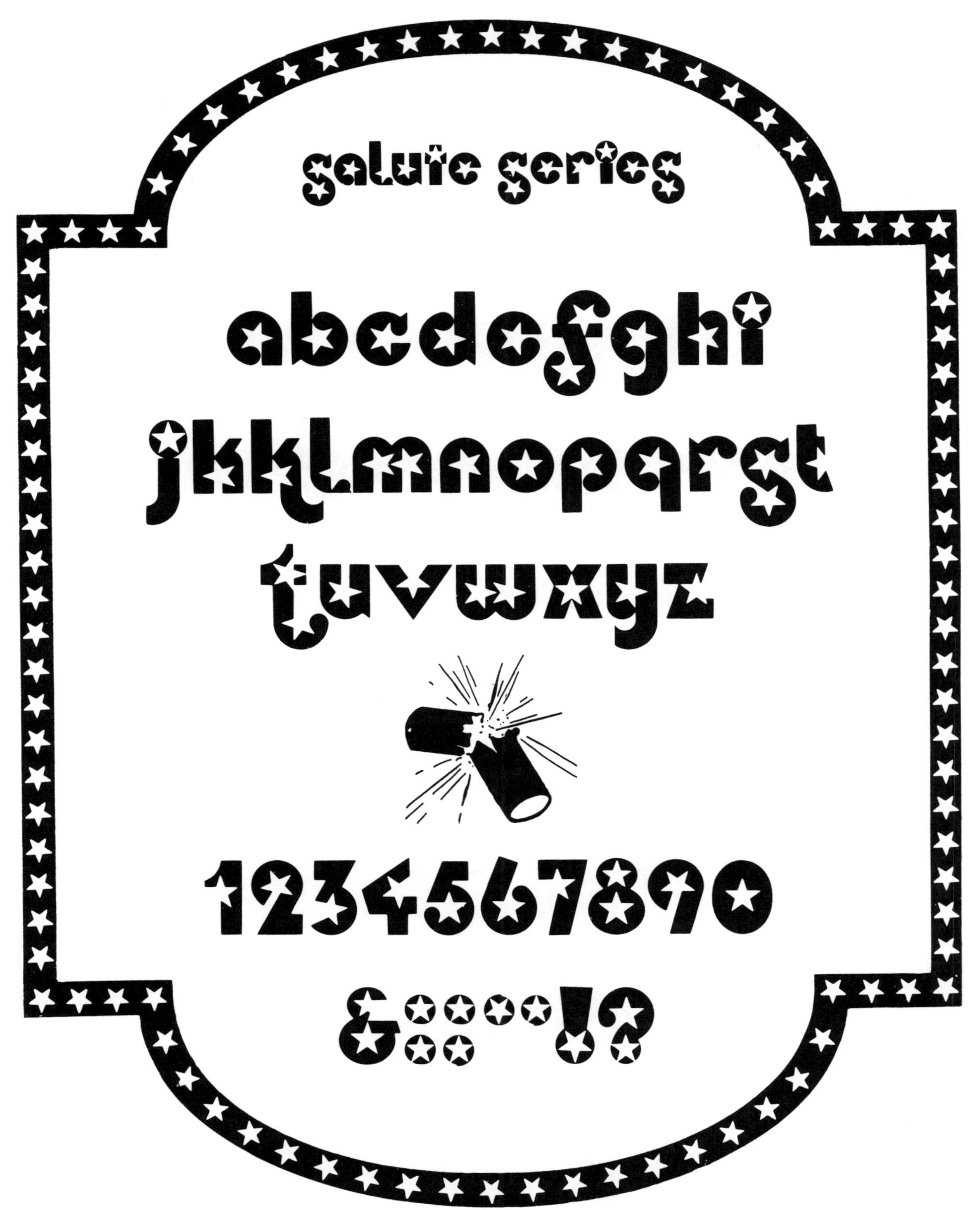
salute series
abcdefghi
jkklmnopqrst
tuvwxyz
1234567890

SCIMITAR

AABCDEFGH
IJKLMNOPQRS
STUVWXYZ

(&.,:;-'£$¢%)

1234567890

SCOREBOARD

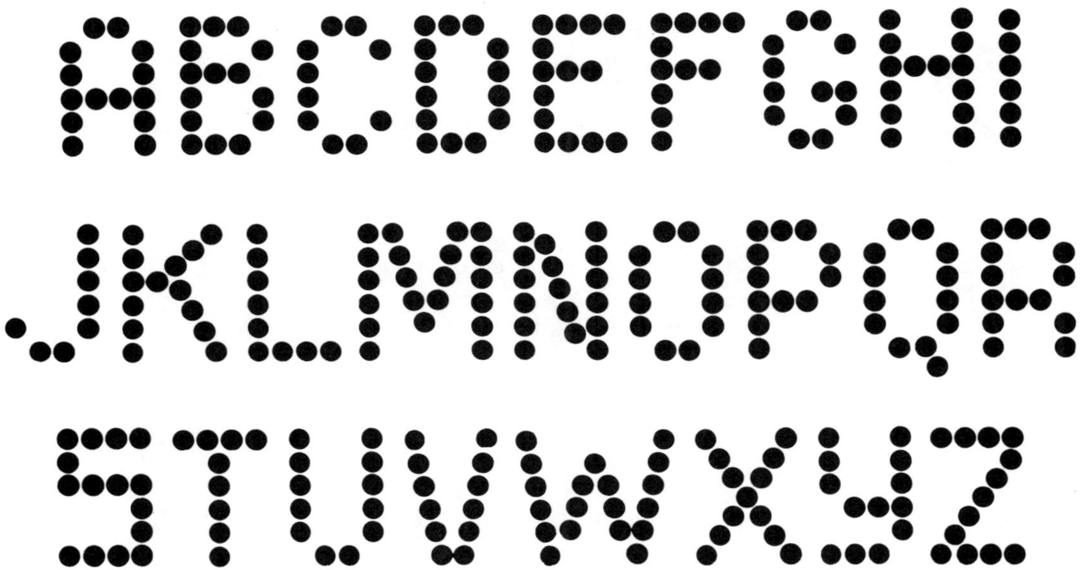

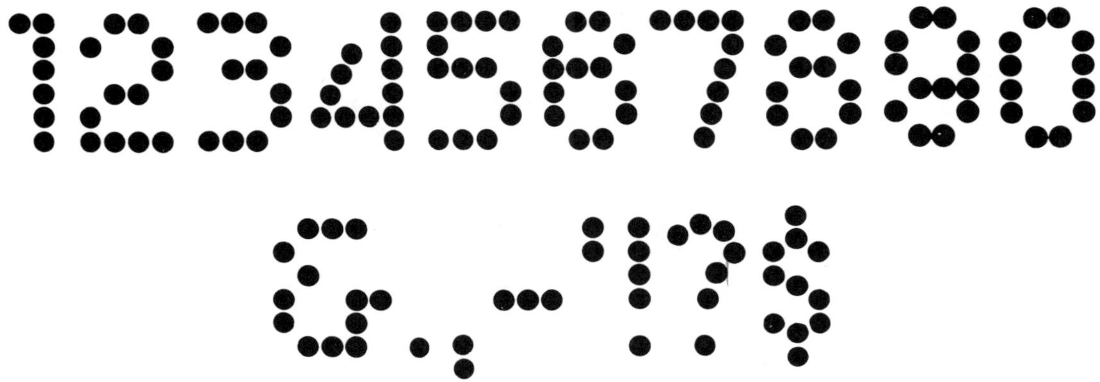

Shalimar

a b c d e f f g

h i j k l m n o p q r

s t u v w x y z

(& : ; - ‘ ’ ? ? ! $)

1 2 3 4 5 6 7 8 9 0

SHALOM

ABCDEF

GHIJKLMN

NOPQRST

UVWXYZ

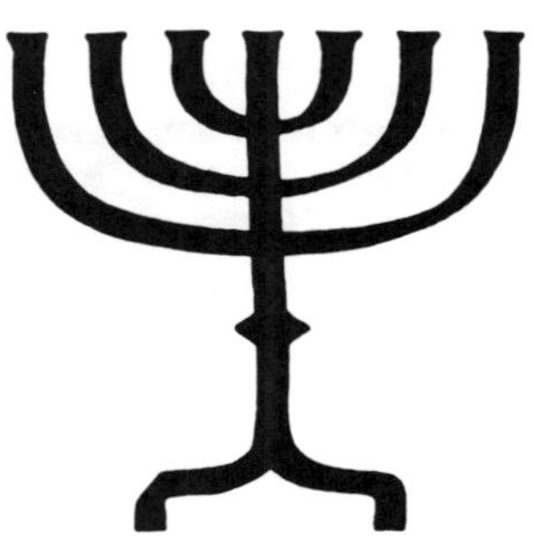

SHANTYTOWN

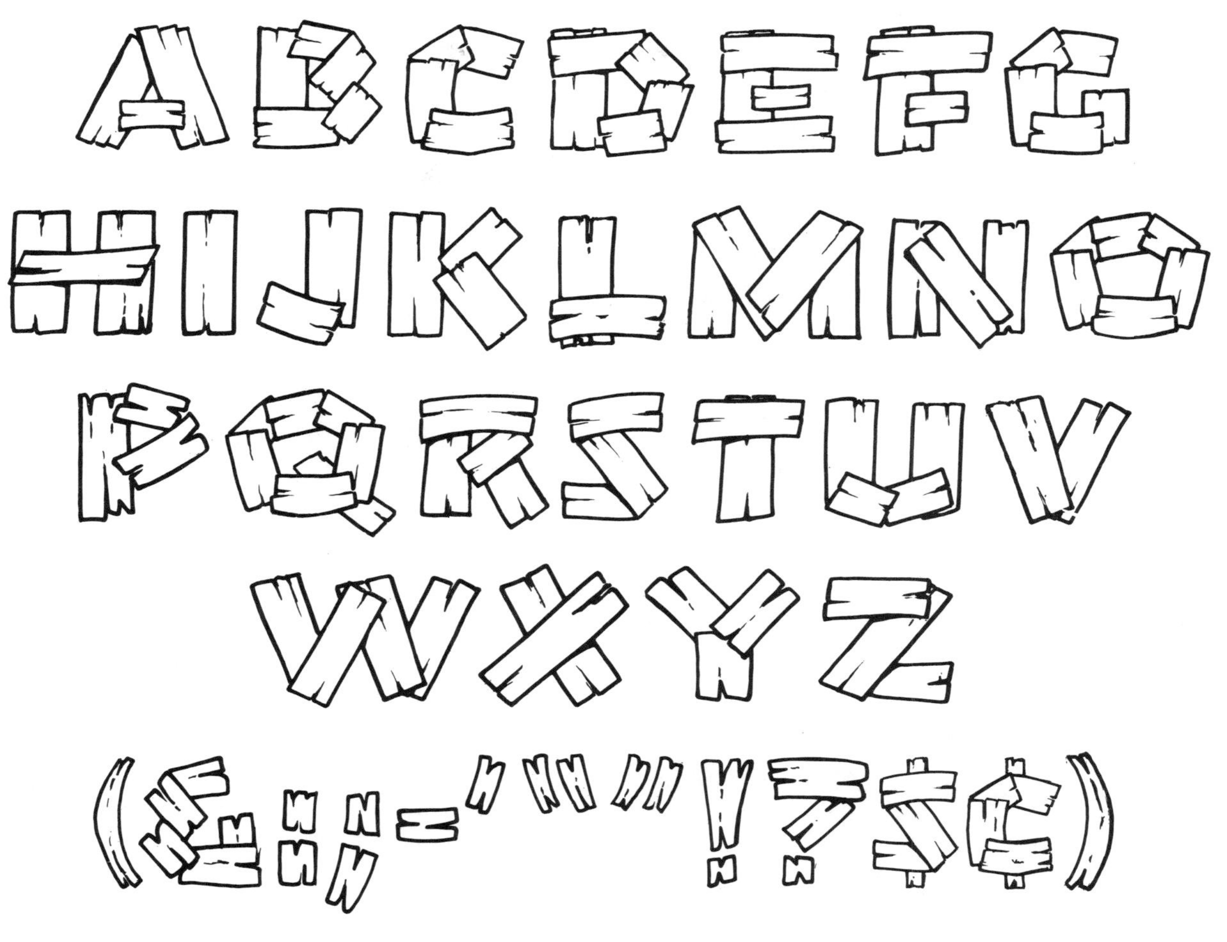

123

4567890

Shatter

ABCDEFGH
IJKLMNOPQR
STUVWXYZ
(&:;-""!?£$)
abcdefghijkl
mnopqrstu
vwxyz
1234567890

abbbcddeef

ghhrijkklmn

noppqqrrss

tuvwwxyyz

siamese

SKYLINE

ABCDEFGHIJ
KLMNOPQRST
UVWXYZ
(&.,;-'"!?$¢%)

1234567890

SLAPSTICK

ABCDEFGHI

JKLMNOPQR

STUVWXYZ

&:;-"!?$¢%

1234567

890

SNOWFLAKE

ABCDEFGHI
JKLMNOPQR
STUVWXYZ

1234567890
:;-'!?$¢

SPLIT CAPS

ABCDEFG
HIJKLMNO
PQRSTUV
WXYZ

(!?.,'$¢)
123456789
0

Square English

ABCDEFGH

IJKLMNOPQR

STUVWXYZ

abcdefghijklmno

pqrstuvwxyz

1234567890

&:;-'!?$¢

STARBURST

ABCDEFGH
IJKLMNO
PQRS
TUVWXYZ
&.,$¢?!
1234567
890

STARS & STRIPES

ABCDEFGH
IJKLMNOPQR
STUVWXYZ

1234567890
(&:;-'!?$¢)

STATIC

ABCDEFGH
IJKLMNOPQR
STUVWXYZ

1234567890
&.,;-'!?$!

Aabcde
fghijklm
nopqrst
uvwxyz
[&.,:;-‘’!?$¢]
1234567
890 Sukiyaki

SUNDOWN

ABCDEFGHIJKLMN

OPQRSTUVWXYZ

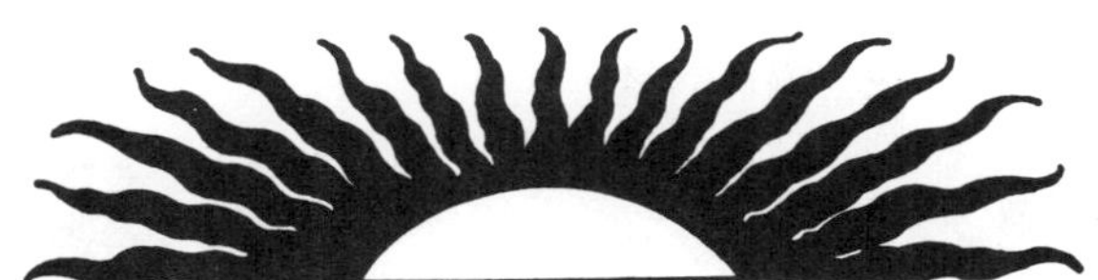

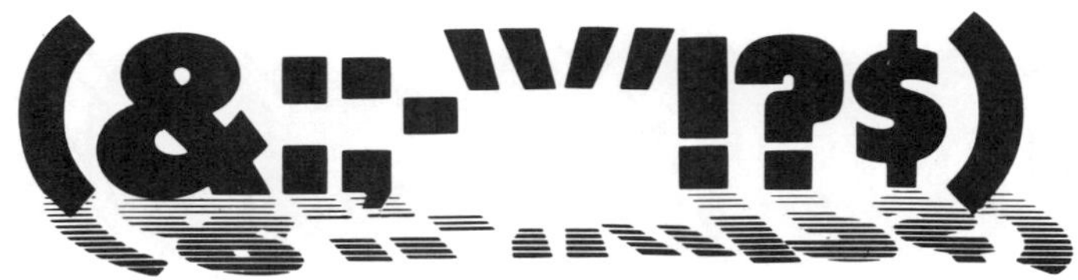

1234567890

TABLEAU

ABCDEFGH

IJKLMNOPQR

STUVWXYZ

& : ; - ' ! ? $ ¢ £

1234567890

Tarantella

ABCDEFGHI
JKLMNOPQR
STUVWXYZ
(&:;!?$¢£)
abcdefghijklm
nopqr
stuvwxyz
1234567890

TARTAN

ABCDEFGH
IJKLMNOP
QRRSSTU
VWXYZST
.,
(&:;!?$)
1234567890

TEACHEST

ABCDEFGHIJKLM

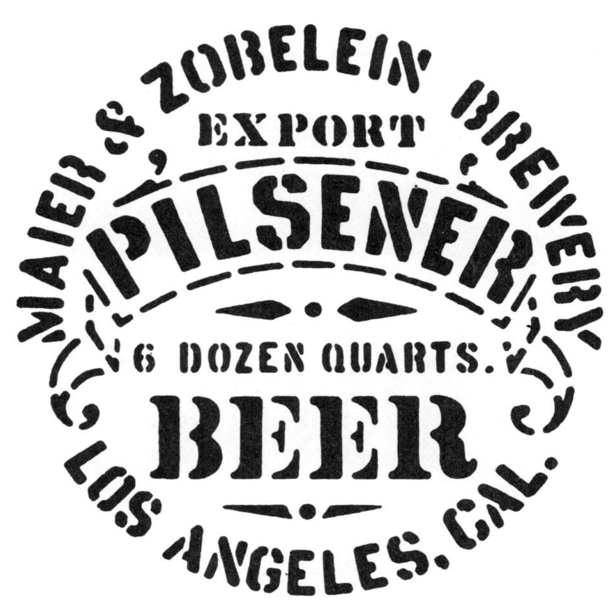

NOPQRSTUVWXYZ

(&:;-“”!?$)

1234567890

TEAM PLAY

ABCDEFGHI

JKLMNOPQR

STUVWXYZ

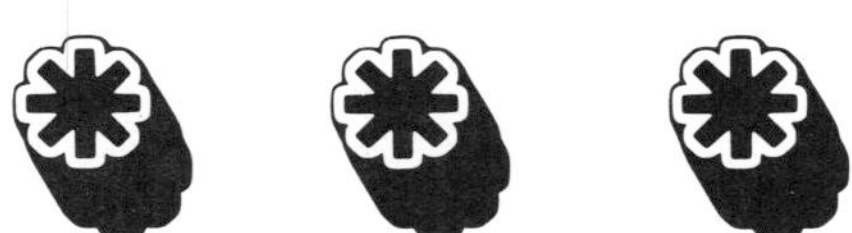

(&:;-'’!?$¢)

1234567890

TENDERLEAF

ABCDEF
GHIJKL
MNOPQ
RSTUV
WXYZ&

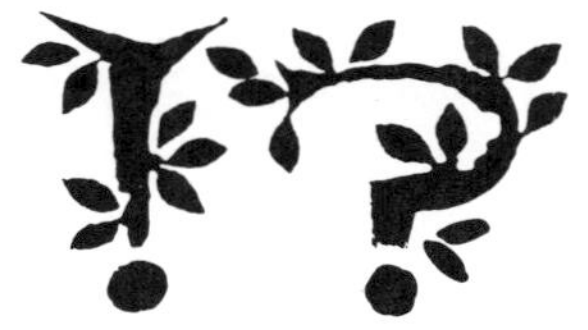

Testemonial Text

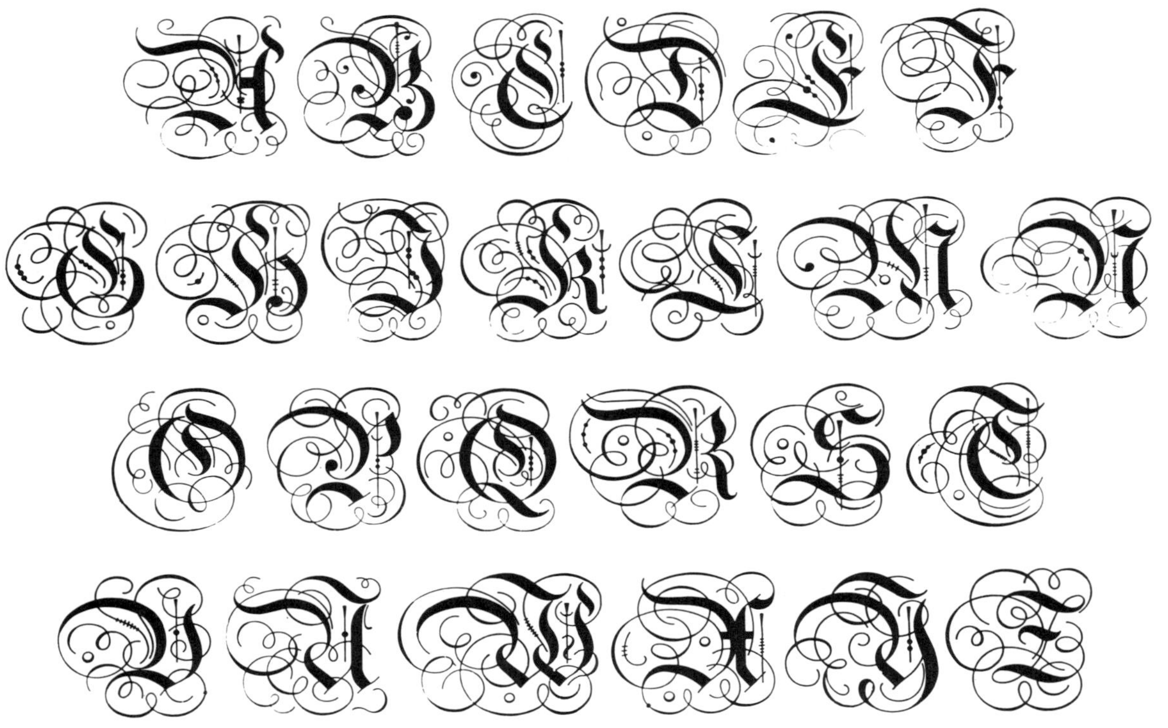

abcdefghijklmn

opqrstuvwxyz

1234567890

(&:;-”“!?$¢£)

timbuctu

aabccdeee_ffg

gghiijkklllmmnn

oopqrrrs

sttuuvwxyyz

&:;-'"''!?$¢

1234567890

TONIGHT

ABCDEFGHI

JKLMNOPQR

STUVWXYZ

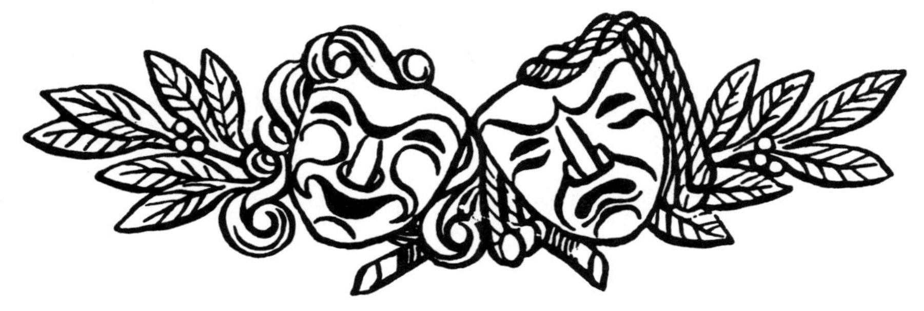

1234567890

(&:;-'’!?$¢)

TRADING STAMP

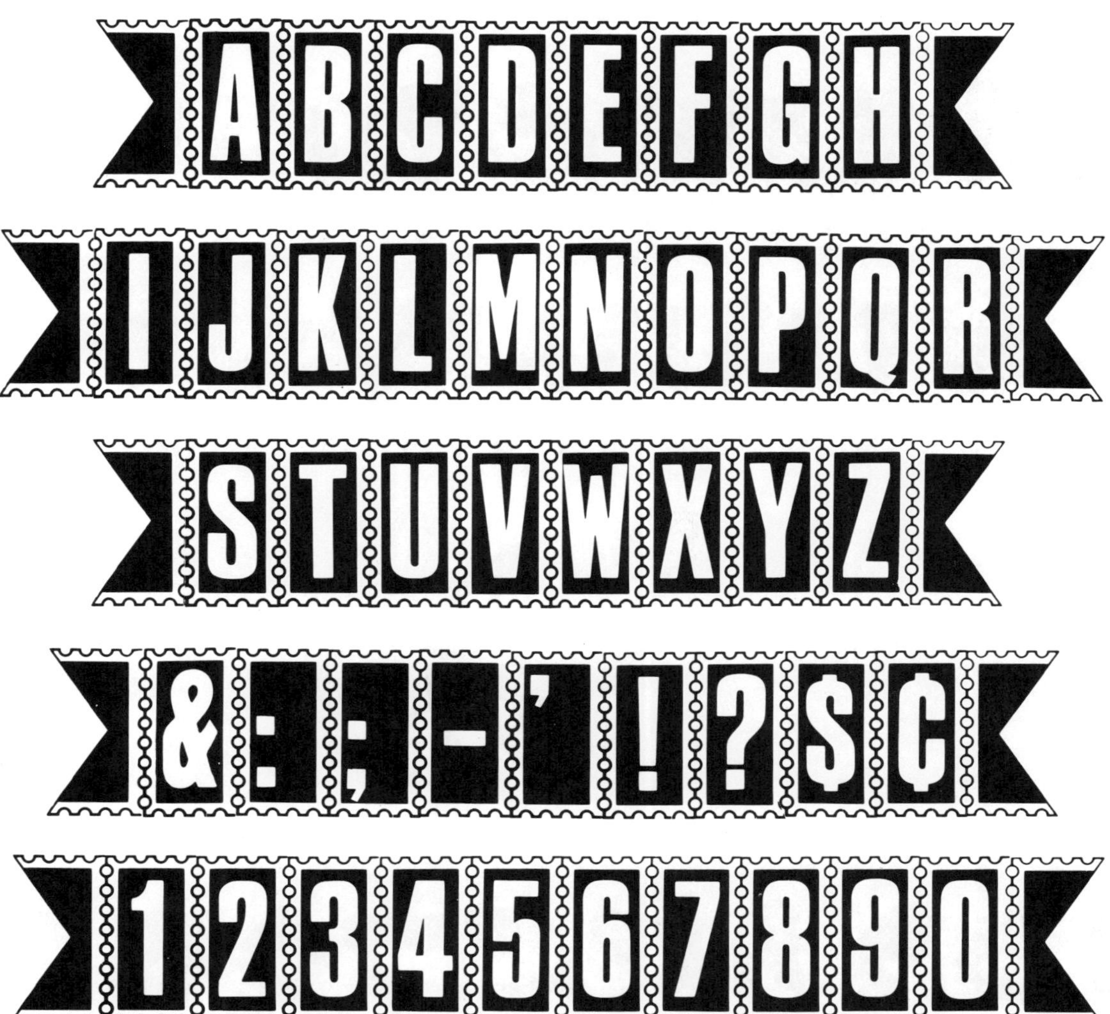

VAMPIRE

ABCDEFGHIJ
KLMNOPQRS
TUVWXYZ

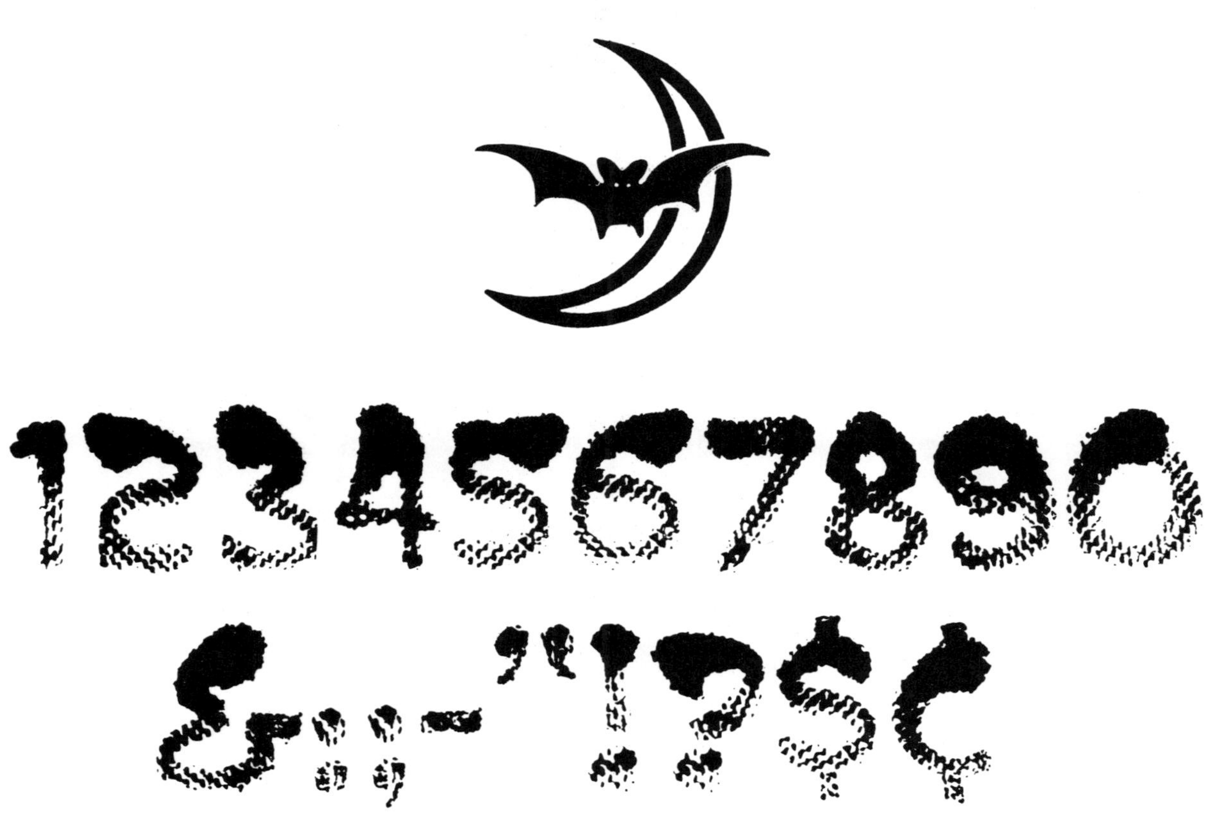

XERXES

ABCDEFGHI

JKLMNOPQRS

TUVWXYZ

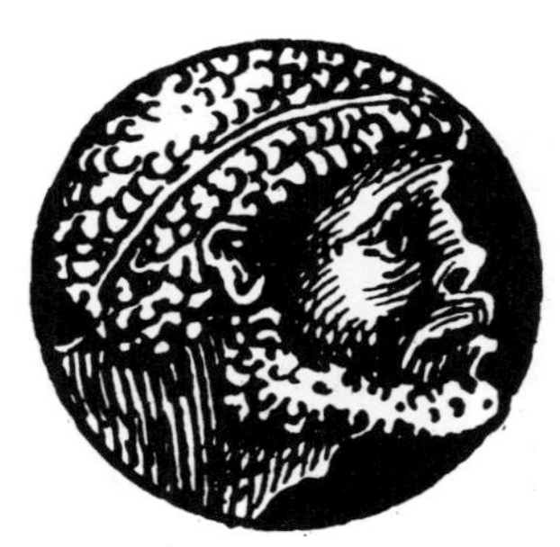

1234567890

(&:;-'?!$¢)

Zebra

ABCDEFG

HIJKLM

NOPQRST

UVWXYZ

(&:;-'!?$£¢)

abcdefghijk

lmnopqrs

tuvwxyz

1234567890